CAMEROON

Sean Sheehan

MARSHALL CAVENDISH
New York • London • Sydney

Reference edition reprinted 2001 by
Marshall Cavendish Corporation
99 White Plains Road
Tarrytown
New York 10591

© Times Media Private Limited 2000

Originated and designed by
Times Books International, an imprint of
Times Media Private Limited, a member of the
Times Publishing Group

All rights reserved. No part of this book may be reproduced or
utilized in any form or by any means electronic or mechanical,
including photocopying, recording, or by an information storage
and retrieval system, without permission from the copyright
owner.

Printed in Malaysia

Library of Congress Cataloging-in-Publication Data:

Sheehan, Sean, 1951–
        Cameroon / Sean Sheehan.
            p. cm. — (Cultures of the World)
        Includes bibliographical references (p.) and index.
        ISBN 0-7614-1158-5
        1. Cameroon—Juvenile literature.   [1. Cameroon.]
I. Title. II. Series.
DT564 .S48 2001
967.11—dc21
                        00–029511
                            CIP
                            AC

INTRODUCTION

THE REPUBLIC OF CAMEROON lies in equatorial, tropical, central-west Africa. Stretching inland from its short Atlantic Ocean coastline to the heart of the African continent, its territory includes a portion of Lake Chad in the north. In this land of mountains, grasslands, and forests live an astonishing variety of cultural groups, numbering over 200, who are finally shaking off a colonial heritage inherited from long periods of foreign rule by France and Britain. Cameroon, one of the few countries in Africa that has managed to evolve from a colony to an independent nation with very little violence, is maturing both economically and politically despite inevitable challenges. This book, in common with the *Cultures of the World* series, sets out to celebrate the Cameroon culture by looking at the way Cameroonians live and work and find enjoyment.

CONTENTS

A man in an elephant mask. The mask is a symbol of power and wealth.

CONTENTS

A Cameroonian girl carrying firewood the African way—by balancing it on her head.

GEOGRAPHY

CAMEROON SHARES ITS BORDERS with a number of other countries: Nigeria to the west, Chad to the northeast, the Central African Republic to the east, and Equatorial Guinea, Gabon, and Congo to the south. Cameroon is not landlocked; it is bordered by the Atlantic Ocean to the southwest, while Lake Chad forms part of its northern border.

FOUR REGIONS

Cameroon has four main geographical regions: the Chad basin, the central plateaus, the western highlands, and the coastal lowlands.

The Chad basin, located at the northern tip of Cameroon, depends on the Logone River and its rich fishing grounds, which provide the main source of food for the people living in the area. The Logone flows for 240 miles (386 km) into the Chari River.

Left: **Crossing Lake Chad in a canoe. Cameroonians often use this mode of water transport.**

Opposite: **Cameroon is well known for its beautiful scenery and natural landmarks such as these prehistoric rocks.**

7

Navigating the Logone River. During the rainy season the area around the Logone becomes very swampy, and floods are common.

The most important feature of central Cameroon is the volcanic upland of the Adamawa Plateau, which extends into eastern Nigeria. The plateau forms the main watershed of Cameroon and has a major influence on the country's weather patterns. It was named after Modibbo Adama, a 19th-century Fulani chief who founded a state in the area. From the plateau, which has an average elevation of 1,969 feet (600 m), a number of major rivers flow into Lake Chad, the Congo Basin, the Gulf of Guinea, and the Niger River in Nigeria. The most important of these rivers is the Bénoué (Benue), a 673-miles-long (1,083-km) tributary of the Niger River. The Bénoué descends about 1,969 feet (600 m) over many rapids. Along the northeastern border, the Logone joins the Chari River, which empties into Lake Chad. There are a number of lower plateaus toward the south, and the steep falls of some of the rivers as they flow to the coast have been exploited to produce hydroelectric power.

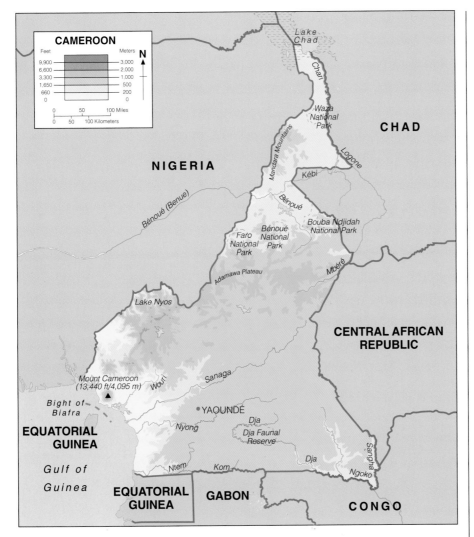

CAMEROON

Feet	Meters
9,900	3,000
6,600	2,000
3,300	1,000
1,650	500
660	200
0	0

0   50   100 Miles
0 50 100 Kilometers

N

When the Tarzan movie Greystoke was being filmed around Mount Cameroon, there was a minor volcanic eruption.

The western highlands, sometimes called the Cameroon Highlands or the grasslands, are an area with volcanic activity, although today the only mountain that is still active is Mount Cameroon (13,440 feet/4,095 m), the only major mountain in West Africa. In the highlands there are numerous volcanic lakes. In 1986 Lake Nyos, a crater lake, released a gas that killed hundreds of people.

The coastal lowlands are characterized by numerous rivers that form swampy areas as they break up into small streams. This provides ideal conditions for mangrove trees, which flourish along parts of the coast.

LAKE NYOS DISASTER

In August 1986 there was a mysterious escape of carbon dioxide gas from Lake Nyos (also spelled Nios) in the mountainous region of western Cameroon near the Nigerian border. The gas, which is odorless, colorless, and heavier than oxygen, flowed downhill from the lake and enveloped a number of small villages. Due to its weight, the gas replaced the oxygen in the air, and more than 1,500 people suffocated as a result. The scientific explanation for this phenomenon is that some kind of volcanic activity below the earth's surface triggered off the release of the gas from the water in which it was pocketed.

MOUNT CAMEROON

Mount Cameroon, *Mont Cameroun* in French, rises to a height of 13,440 feet (4,095 m) and is situated 14 miles (23 km) inland from the Gulf of Guinea. Mount Cameroon is the highest peak in sub-Saharan western and central Africa. The port of Limbe, formerly called Victoria, lies at the southern foot of the mountain. The sea-facing side of the mountain has a reputation for being one of the wettest parts of Cameroon, with more than 394 inches (1,000 cm) of rain every year. In 1861 the English explorer Sir Richard Francis Burton (1821–90) was the first European to climb to the top. Still active, the volcanic Mount Cameroon last erupted in 1959.

Many people still live and work near the foot of Mount Cameroon despite its volcanic eruptions.

CLIMATE

For an equatorial country, Cameroon has a surprisingly variable climate. This is due to a number of local factors that affect weather patterns. Cameroon has a tropical climate, which means that the main seasons are not summer and winter but wet and dry periods. Around Douala on the coast, the rainy period often lasts seven months. This area has over 169 inches (430 cm) of rain a year. In the Chad basin, the wet season lasts only a couple of months and annual rainfall is only 32 inches (80 cm).

Altitude affects the temperature, so there can be huge differences in average temperatures even within the same area. Coastal regions with an altitude of 2,954 feet (900 m) record average temperatures of 68°F (20°C) while Douala, which is at sea level, has an average of 79°F (26°C).

The harmattan, a dry, hot wind that blows from the Sahara desert during the dry months, also affects the climate. The wind carries with it sand and dust from the desert, and this adds to the aridity; thus the north of the country, which is nearer to the Sahara, has a longer dry season.

Indigenous people in the southern rainforest during the rainy season. Nearer the coast the wet season broadly extends from April to November, and the dry period lasts from December to March.

11

The **Waza National Park** *(right)*, **where savanna animals such as lions** *(above)*, **monkeys, baboons, and white pelicans make their home, lies in northern Cameroon.**

FORESTS AND GRASSLANDS

The combination of different temperatures and rainfall produces two major types of vegetation in Cameroon: equatorial forest and tropical grassland. Rainforest and mangrove swamps are found near the coast, where rainfall is highest. Mangrove trees anchor themselves in swampy water by means of long, spreading roots that reveal their architecture when the tide is out and their complex root system is exposed on the mud banks. The hardwood rainforest consists of mahogany, ebony, sapelli, iroko, and obeche trees, which may grow to more than 200 feet (61 m). Because of their economic value, the rainforests have been extensively logged.

Moving inland from the coast, rainfall decreases and the forest thins out. A mix of forest and grassland then gives way to savanna, where

trees and bushes are few. Acacia and baobab trees survive here because they can shed their leaves and prolong their ability to survive dry periods. There are a few hundred species of acacia trees in Cameroon, and one of them produces the dye that was the original source of khaki coloring. The large and impressive-looking baobab tree is distinguished by its massive trunk, which is part of the tree's water-storage system. There is a rich variety of grasses growing in Cameroon's savanna belt, some of the tallest can grow to over 6 feet (2 m) in height. Evergreen trees and papyrus grass thrive along the river banks, benefiting from their close proximity to water.

This variety in vegetation, plus regional factors such as the presence of rich volcanic soil around Mount Cameroon and other parts of the western highlands, accounts for the diverse agricultural potential of the country.

Lake Tison, surrounded by a dense forest, is located about 6 miles (10 km) from Ngaoundéré.

FLORA AND FAUNA

Cameroon has a wonderfully diverse flora and fauna. It is not difficult to imagine a time in the future when far more tourists will be visiting the country to appreciate the wildlife and the many rare species of plants and animals. Elephants, crocodiles, rhinoceroses, hippopotamuses, lions, panthers, cheetahs, and gorillas are found in Cameroon, though the numbers are not significant. Less spectacular are palm-spiders, which grow as big as a saucer. Warthogs, one of the world's endangered animals, are still to be found in the more remote forests. Another rare animal is the drill, a large baboon with a short tail. It has a red lower lip, brown fur, and theatrically-colored buttocks.

Baby chimpanzees in the Waza National Park.

RESOURCES

Petroleum was discovered in the Gulf of Guinea in the mid 1970s, and crude oil was first produced in 1977. Cameroon does not rank as a world player in the international oil market, but its oil industry makes a valuable contribution to the country's economy because it accounts for over half of the total annual exports.

There is tremendous potential for hydroelectric power, and existing dams and hydroelectric stations provide a substantial amount of electricity for towns and cities.

Limestone and a kind of rock called pozzolana, used in the making of cement, are found in plentiful supply in Cameroon. The country also benefits from deposits of bauxite, diamonds, and iron ore, but these are not yet commercially exploited on a large scale.

Apart from crude oil, African oil palm is another of Cameroon's exports.

15

Douala is the only town in Cameroon with an industrial base, and over three-quarters of the country's industrial activity take place here.

CITIES

The creation and development of many towns in Cameroon can be traced back to the country's colonial era. A settlement on the coast at Douala existed when the first European traders arrived in this part of West Africa, but it was under German colonial rule that the place developed into the country's largest port.

During their rule, the Germans established a trading station at Yaoundé to keep out their French and British trading rivals. No large villages existed in the Yaoundé area until a fort was built and a telegraph station established. It then developed into an administrative center for trade, and mission schools were established. Gradually it grew to become the country's capital city. Yaoundé remains very much an administrative and educational center.

Other important cities include Bamenda, Bafoussam, and Nkongsamba, which are located in the more densely populated western part of the country. Most towns in Cameroon are growing rapidly, especially in the west as many people are migrating to the cities from nearby rural areas. Since most Cameroonians are not wealthy, the increasing number of people moving to urban areas is creating shantytowns where the level of housing is inadequate and basic facilities such as running water and electricity are in short supply.

Limbe, situated on the coast at the southern foot of Mount Cameroon, is Cameroon's second largest port. Coffee, cocoa, palm oil, tea, bananas, and rubber are exported through Limbe. Originally christened Victoria, in honor of Queen Victoria of Britain, the town was founded in 1858 by Baptist missionaries. Limbe now has a population of over 50,000, and its colonial-style architecture is waiting to be discovered by a new generation of tourists.

The University of Yaoundé is the only institution of higher education in the country. It was founded in 1962.

17

HISTORY

LITTLE IS KNOWN ABOUT THE HISTORY of Cameroon before colonization in the 19th century. This is partly because the country did not yet exist as a nation state, and up to A.D. 1500, none of the great kingdoms that rose to power in West Africa were based in what is now Cameroon. Since the country came into existence, its history has been a remarkably stable one.

BEFORE COLONIALISM

Before the 1880s there was no one state covering the area known today as Cameroon. Instead there were numerous small states, each of which had its own cultural identity and history. Migration of people between one state and another was common and usually dictated by shifting patterns of economic relationships. Bantu-speakers from equatorial Africa are the first people known to have invaded the south and west of the country, and in the 18th and 19th centuries, Muslim Fulani people moved into the north of Cameroon.

The first Europeans to navigate down the west coast of Africa as far as the Gulf of Guinea were the Portuguese explorers in the 15th century. In 1472 the first Portuguese ships entered the estuary of the Wouri river and were surprised at the plenitude of prawns in the coastal creeks. The name of the country was then created from the Portuguese word for prawns, *camaroes* ("CA-mah-row"), though it was later called Camerones by the Spanish, Kamerun by the Germans, Cameroun by the French, and Cameroon by the British.

Above: **A prehistoric fossil stone found in northern Cameroon.**

Opposite: **The Bandjoun Palace, about 12 miles (20 km) from Bafoussam, is a fine example of traditional Bamiléké architecture.**

SLAVE TRADE

In the late 18th century Cameroon and the delta area of the Niger River were the focal point for the transport of slaves. An estimated 20,000 men and women left these shores every year.

The slave trade developed a trading network that was later used to transport commercial goods when the slave trade ended. The slaves or goods were traded or stolen inland and then passed along through a series of middlemen until they reached the coast where European trading ships waited offshore.

As the demand for slaves increased due to the need for labor on plantations in South, Central, and North America, the slave trade became big business. Many African traders became rich by organizing large slave-hunting expeditions in the interior.

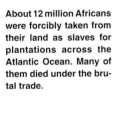

About 12 million Africans were forcibly taken from their land as slaves for plantations across the Atlantic Ocean. Many of them died under the brutal trade.

GERMAN COLONIALISM

The closing decades of the 19th century witnessed a struggle between European powers for lucrative new colonies in Africa as a growing demand for natural resources in Europe made it profitable for them to take possession of a part of Africa and treat it as an extension of their own state. This became known as the "scramble for Africa." The Douala people, living around the Wouri River, signed a treaty in July 1884 that permitted German rule in the area close to the river. Palm oil, rubber, tobacco, tea, coffee, bananas, and cocoa were all valuable products worth exporting, so the Germans eventually expanded their rule inland by setting up routes to their plantations. This brought the colonists into conflict with the local traders, who until then had always traded with Europeans on the coast. Violence broke out whenever the locals resisted.

A coffee farmer setting off to harvest the beans. Coffee remains till this day one of the major export crops of Cameroon.

The period of German colonialism only lasted from 1884 to 1916, but it was a very decisive period because for the first time, a boundary was established around the region that would evolve into Cameroon. Mission schools were set up by Germans and eventually produced a small elite group of literate clerks, pastors, and teachers. The Germans also gave a name to their new territory on the west coast of Africa—Kamerun. Douala was developed as the main port, and new settlements were founded inland.

World War I, which broke out in 1914, was partially a struggle between European superpowers to gain control of profitable imperial possessions. Kamerun, a land rich in natural resources, was invaded by French and British armies. When the war ended in 1918 with the defeat of Germany, Kamerun was divided between the victors. Under a League of Nations mandate, the larger share of the territory, about four-fifths of Kamerun, went to France and became French Cameroon. A smaller area in the west that bordered Nigeria went to Britain. The country was thus divided in two. The British territory was itself split into British Southern Cameroon and British Northern Cameroon.

THE FIRST REBELS

Toward the end of their colonial rule, the Germans set about segregating Douala into separate white and black areas, as well as forcibly removing inhabitants. This was an extremely racist act, with an economic motive. The German authorities had wanted to own the land that was becoming increasingly valuable without having to pay the local landowners market price for it. Opposition to the segregation was organized under the leadership of Rudolph Manga Bell, who was later put on trial for treason and executed. On the day that he died, in 1914, another rebel also faced a firing squad, Martin-Paul Samba, for offering to help the French if they would remove German rule.

A SHARED COUNTRY

A monument in Douala honoring French forces.

As the British sector was attached to Nigeria, a larger and more valuable part of the British Empire, many thousands of Nigerians moved into south Cameroon. In British Cameroon the English language was used in schools and the administration, while French was used in the rest of the country. Neither imperial power was particularly interested in encouraging their nationals to settle in Cameroon. Their main interest was to exploit the land's economic possibilities and develop plantations, especially for coffee.

Meanwhile Douala developed in importance as a major port, and a small but significant number of industrial concerns were set up in the area close to the coast, including a hydroelectric plant and an aluminum-processing plant. After World War II these developments attracted an increased number of Europeans to Cameroon and, because the Europeans were offered better employment opportunities, racial tensions began to develop. The sense of nationalism among Cameroonians grew.

NATIONALISM

The influx of Nigerians into British Cameroon, where many of them held minor positions of power in the police force and the judiciary, led to the feeling that Cameroon was a colony of a colony. This strengthened calls for reunification of the two parts of the country. In French Cameroon a labor organization, the Union des Populations du Cameroun (UPC), went underground and called for active resistance to French rule. In 1956 a form of self-government was introduced by France. The colonial power remained in control of foreign policy, and a coalition government was established. This government fell from power in 1958, and a second coalition government was formed under the leadership of Ahmadou Ahidjo. There were now calls for complete independence, and Ahidjo's government offered an amnesty to UPC nationalists, who agreed to cease their guerilla war against the French administration.

INDEPENDENCE FOR FRENCH CAMEROON

French Cameroon gained independence on January 1, 1960, and the Republic of Cameroon came into existence. It was not known at the time, but agreements had been made to preserve French economic and military interests to ensure a peaceful transition to independence.

There was no constitution when Ahidjo became ruler of the country in 1960. He consolidated his own power and tailored a constitution that suited the interests of the government and the people that he represented. New elections took place four months after independence, and although the UPC was allowed to take part, Ahidjo's party won 51 out of the 100 seats. Ahidjo himself stood for election as president and, being the only candidate, he was successfully elected. His party sought to avoid open conflict and formed a coalition government with all the parties except the UPC.

Below: **A congregation of Cameroonians. It has been estimated that the lives of about 600 rebels and over 1,000 police and government officials were lost in the struggle for independence. Around 15,000 civilians were killed, and almost twice that number were driven from their homes.**

Opposite: **Ahmadou Ahidjo, the first president of Cameroon.**

COMPLETE INDEPENDENCE

Below: **Cameroonians have enjoyed peace and stability since independence.**

Opposite: **President Ahidjo and officials at the opening of a health center.**

In British Cameroon before 1960, there were calls for reunification with French Cameroon, but there were also calls by other groups for a merger with Nigeria. The British rulers gradually allowed greater autonomy to Cameroon representatives in the Nigerian federal government. In 1961 a plebiscite was held, and voters were given the choice between unification with Nigeria or with the new Republic of Cameroon. The result for British Southern Cameroon was overwhelmingly in favor of reunification with the former French Cameroon. British Northern Cameroon chose to join Nigeria. In October 1961 the Federal Republic of Cameroon came into existence, uniting the South British and French areas into one new country.

THE AHIDJO YEARS

Ahmadou Ahidjo was the undisputed leader of Cameroon's government until 1982. He was a dictator, personally governing nearly all aspects of political life. He began by forming a single political party, the Cameroon National Union (CNU), in the French-influenced eastern part of the country and merging it with a number of different parties in the British-influenced west of the country. Parties that failed to cooperate with this process were outlawed and their leaders arrested. In theory it was possible for new political parties to be formed, but in reality it was extremely difficult and no new party was allowed to develop an effective voice. Military force was used to destroy the remnants of the UPC opposition to the new state. Labor unions were forced to form a single organization, which then came under the political control of the government.

State power became centralized in Yaoundé, and previous forms of local government were dismantled. In 1972 the federal system of government was abolished and the country became the United Republic of Cameroon. A number of provinces were created, each one ruled by a governor and regional officers. All government officials were appointed by Ahidjo.

Below: **Workers in an aluminium factory. Most factories prospered during Ahidjo's rule.**

Opposite: **President Paul Biya making an address at the UN General Assembly on the 50th anniversary of the founding of the United Nations.**

Cameroon was under a political, not military, dictatorship because Ahidjo was able to use his position to win cooperation from individuals and groups who might otherwise have mounted opposition to his rule. At the same time it was generally known that political opposition to Ahidjo would not be tolerated, and human rights such as press freedom were severely restricted and controlled.

Ahidjo's ability to single-handedly rule his country was aided by the financial support of the French government and the commercial backing to his regime that came from the powerful business interests that remained largely under French control. At a more local level Ahidjo was able to distribute jobs and contracts to people who would support him.

The civil service went through a process of "Cameroonization," replacing French officials with Cameroonians; this helped to ensure loyalty to the government.

THE BIYA YEARS

President Ahidjo resigned in 1982 and handed power over to his prime minister, Paul Biya. A peaceful and voluntary transfer of power in Africa is not a very common event, and it was commonly felt at the time that Ahidjo did not intend to relinquish all his power. But Biya emerged as an independent leader who was not willing to act as a puppet for Ahidjo. In 1983 the resignation of Ahidjo as president of the CNU and his replacement by Biya signaled a decisive shift of power. A plot against the government was said to have been discovered, and there were rumors that Ahidjo was implicated in this.

Once in power, Biya announced the need for a more democratic form of government. Ahidjo, who left the country for France, was found guilty of involvement in a plot to take over the government and was sentenced to death. Although this sentence was later reduced, it prompted another coup attempt in 1984, and an estimated 1,000 people were killed before the rebellion was crushed.

GOVERNMENT

OVER THE YEARS OF ITS EXISTENCE, Cameroon has had a remarkably stable government, though for much of that time, it has been one-party rule. The first constitution of 1961 was changed in 1972 when the United Republic of Cameroon was formed. Executive powers remained in the hands of the president, who is the head of the government and chief of the armed forces. He is also responsible for appointing all the ministers. The president is elected for a period of five years by direct and secret universal suffrage. Legislative power is held by a National Assembly of 180 members, elected for five-year terms. The republic is divided into 10 provinces, each administered by a governor. Each province is divided into departments.

STARTING FROM SCRATCH

When Cameroon became an independent state in 1961, there was a need to create a constitution and a form of government. A sense of identity to unite all Cameroonians over and above the various ethnic loyalties that divided citizens of the new state had to be created too. In particular, people from the British and French areas of influence and people from the northern and southern parts of the country had to be brought together to live in harmony. Without some sense of shared identity, there was a danger that the nation would fall apart.

Such problems faced many newly emerging African states in the 1960s. Many of them, like Cameroon, had been shaped and defined by colonial experiences that had never nurtured national identity. In many cases, including Cameroon, the physical boundaries of the state had been artificially created by colonial powers, and the national territory had forced together different ethnic groups with their own languages and cultures. Such a situation gave new governments an excuse to create authoritarian political systems, and this is what happened in Cameroon.

Opposite: **Ahmadou Ahidjo had been president of Cameroon for 22 years when he stepped down in 1982.**

AHIDJO'S GOVERNMENT

From independence until 1982 Cameroon was governed by Ahmadou Ahidjo because he created a presidential system of government that invested nearly all the powers of state in his own position as the president.

The constitution was altered so that the president became the head of state, the head of government, and the commander of military forces. The National Assembly had no executive powers and simply rubber-stamped whatever legislation the president proposed. Ministers, governors, and judges were all appointed by the president. When elections of the National Assembly took place, the party that received the majority of votes automatically won all the available seats. This made it virtually impossible for any new party to win representation in the assembly because they would have to obtain over 50% of all votes in the country. Thus the CNU always remained in power.

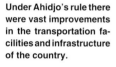

Under Ahidjo's rule there were vast improvements in the transportation facilities and infrastructure of the country.

AHMADOU AHIDJO

Ahmadou Ahidjo was born in Cameroon in 1924 and died an exile in 1989 after being sentenced to death for alleged involvement in an antigovernment coup. He served as president for over 20 years, and although he insisted on retaining power strictly for himself and his own party, he kept his country free of the internal power struggles that destabilized the other African nations that gained their independence around the same time. His greatest achievement was to successfully and peacefully oversee the emergence of Cameroon as one united country, formed from two separate and not always harmonious states. A Muslim from northern Cameroon, he maintained control and stability with the active support of the French government.

BIYA'S GOVERNMENT

When Biya gained power in 1982, he announced the need for more democracy and changed the constitution to allow non-CNU members to stand in presidential elections. There was still no opposition, however, when Biya won the presidential election in 1984. The centralization of power in the hands of the president remained intact. What had changed was the new president's willingness to use that power to bring about some relaxation in the dictatorial state, and his promise to introduce democratic reforms.

There were important changes in the running of government ministries. People were appointed because of their skill and aptitude for the job and not just their political usefulness to the president. In 1987 Biya wrote a book entitled *Communal Liberalism* in which he explained the kind of government he wanted to bring about and the need for the "establishment of a new political society." He also made it clear that although a multiparty state was a goal to aim for, it would be necessary to maintain one-party rule for the time being.

Biya also announced the need for a National Charter of Freedom, a defined set of human rights that would apply to all Cameroonians. Although press censorship still exists today, it is felt that more freedom is allowed under Biya than was ever possible under Ahidjo.

Under Biya the United Republic of Cameroon became simply the Republic of Cameroon, on the grounds that the people had become united, and so there was no further need for the word "United."

NEW PARTIES

Cameroon was a one-party state from 1966 and was dominated by the CNU. In 1985 the CNU became the Cameroon People's Democratic Movement (RDPC). A change of name was not enough to persuade people that the governing party was interested in serious democratic reforms, and the second half of the 1980s witnessed political unrest and violent clashes between government forces and groups calling for political change. In 1990 a constitutional amendment established a multiparty system, although the RDPC remained dominant. Other constitutional reforms in 1993 sought to decentralize the government. The main opposition is the Social Democratic Front, which challenged Biya for the presidency.

When Ahidjo resigned, a major economic crisis was developing in Cameroon. The crisis arose because of declining world prices for commodities. President Biya *(below),* **however, was unfairly blamed for it.**

THE JUDICIARY

Cameroon has a Higher Judicial Council that is constitutionally responsible, along with the president, for guaranteeing the independence of the judiciary. The role of the council is to advise the president on the nomination of magistrates and judges and monitor the performance of their duties.

The legal system of Cameroon consists of the Supreme Court, two courts of appeal, high courts, and circuit courts. The Supreme Court has the power to decide whether a bill should come before the National Assembly if there is a dispute between the president and the legislature. There is also a Court of Impeachment that can pass judgment on the president in cases of high treason and on other government ministers in the event of a coup against the government.

A government building in the capital of Cameroon, Yaoundé.

CHIEFS

Before colonialism the power of government operated through a system of chiefs. Each chief or *fon* ("FOND") had his own special hut and, depending on local politics, had a number of more powerful chiefs he had to submit to, or smaller chiefs that he could rule. The chief combined the powers of judge and jury for his own village, leading to the view that the chief was an autocratic ruler with dictatorial powers. This is, however, not true in most cases. Many chiefs governed with the assistance of a council of older and more respected members of the community, and this acted as a modifying force to the chief's unilateral powers.

Today chiefs no longer hold any official political power, although it is not uncommon for a chief to hold a local government post. Official or not, chiefs still have an important social influence.

The beautifully painted walls of a village chief's house. In rural areas the house of the village chief is usually larger than that of anyone else.

INTERNATIONALISM

Cameroon has a longstanding and important relationship with France, since part of the country used to be a French colony. At the time of independence, France played an important role in shaping the government that emerged, and still exerts an influence on the land it once controlled. The two countries have economic, diplomatic, military, and cultural links, and together they strengthen and preserve a relationship that was forged in the era of colonialism. Critics sometimes argue that Cameroon is still too closely tied to its old colonial master because the economic and military links encourage a relationship of dependency. Nevertheless, Cameroon has developed friendly relations, both economic and diplomatic, with other nations both within and outside of Europe. Cameroon's historical ties to Britain account for the country's membership in the Commonwealth.

President Biya *(left)* paying a visit to Germany after the disastrous volcanic gas eruption at Lake Nyos in 1986. Here he shakes hands with Helmut Kohl, foreign minister of Germany. The president of Germany had promised to provide aid to Cameroon.

RECENT ELECTIONS

Biya was elected to another term of office as president in the October 1997 election, receiving over 92% of the 4 million votes cast. Elections for the National Assembly took place in May 1997, and the RDPC won 109 of the 180 seats. The Social Democratic Front won 43 seats; the National Union for Democracy and Progress 13 seats; the Democratic Union of Cameroon five seats; and three seats were won by independent candidates. The remaining seven seats were considered void by the Supreme Court because of allegations of vote rigging.

ECONOMY

CAMEROON IS PROUD that the country has enough resources to feed its people. Self-sufficiency in food distinguishes it from many other African states. Cameroon also has an enviable reputation for economic stability, and its market-oriented policies encourage foreign investment. Its economy accounts for half the Gross Domestic Product (GDP) of all the countries of Central Africa combined. On the downside the encouragement of a free market has produced problems, such as corruption and the destruction of Cameroon's forests for short-term gain. For much of the 1990s, there was no economic growth, and the country's dependence on the World Bank and the International Monetary Fund means that its economic policies are largely directed by these institutions. This explains the government's current policy to privatize many sectors of the economy. These policies have led to economic hardship for the people of Cameroon.

Left: **A currency note of Cameroon.**

Opposite: **A man selling hats along a street in Ngaoundéré.**

A couple rolling a ball of cotton. Cameroon produces around 200,000 tons (181,400 metric tons) of cotton each year, allowing it to compete with Chad as the main cotton producer in Central Africa.

AGRICULTURE

Three out of four Cameroonians live and work on their own land, producing around 90% of the country's food. The economy is heavily dependent on agriculture. The average size of a farmstead is small, around 7 acres (3 hectares), but this is still adequate to maintain a lifestyle that is reasonably self-sufficient. Cash crops include coffee, bananas, peanuts, palm oil, and cocoa.

In the north farmers primarily grow grain and raise animals. In the south there is more variety in the farming: millet, rice, groundnuts, maize, and cassava are grown, and cattle, goats, sheep, and horses raised. Lake Chad and the rivers flowing into it provide a rich supply of fish. On the plateaus farther south, the conditions are suitable for growing cotton, cocoa, coffee, and tobacco. Cameroon is the fifth largest producer of cocoa in the world.

The altitude and climate of the western highlands is ideal for planting coffee, maize, groundnuts, and plantains. The forested area in the south, where cattle cannot be raised, produces more cocoa than any other region.

TRADE

The colonial legacy is felt in most aspects of Cameroonian life, and the economy is no exception. When the country gained independence, around 60% of exports went to France. This has gradually dropped to 25% in recent years. Although Cameroon has developed trading ties with other countries, France still supplies more than one-third of total imports. Other important trading partners are Holland, Spain, and Germany. Trade with other African and Arab countries has also increased.

Cameroon's major exports are crude oil, coffee, cocoa, cotton, tea, rubber, peanuts, bananas, aluminium, and timber. Imports consist mainly of industrial and household goods, motor vehicles and other transport equipment, as well as spare parts, fertilizers, and pesticides.

Although the majority of citizens are still practicing subsistence farming, more businesses have sprouted over the years. Cameroon is on its way to becoming a capitalist state operating on the basis of private enterprise and the free flow of capital.

Logging in Yaoundé. Forestry in Cameroon is limited to the more accessible areas around the Douala-Yaoundé railway and the main roads.

FOREST DESTRUCTION

Cameroon produces more logs than any country in Africa, and this results in very few virgin forests remaining. Given that Cameroon has one of the largest tropical forests in the continent, this has depressing consequences for the environment and wildlife of the region. Experts believe that Cameroon is exploiting this resource at a faster rate than it can be sustained through replanting, and the long-term result of this will be the total destruction of a valuable and precious resource.

Part of the problem arises from concessions sold to individual companies to exploit an area of forest. The problem of corruption is not well-controlled in Cameroon, and this means that the more unscrupulous companies—the ones that pay the highest bribes—are often more likely to gain logging contracts. This tends to sideline the more responsible companies, leaving corrupt ones with the opportunity to abuse their position by excessive logging with little regard for replanting and conservation.

DEPLETION OF FORESTS

A commercial company intent on maximizing its profits does not look at a forest in the same way as a conservation group. Conservationists look at the forest as a whole, seeking to preserve its ecological identity and understand that any one area of a forest contains different types of trees growing in harmony. From a narrow commercial point of view, it makes sense to select and log only the most valuable trees in an area. It has been estimated that 10% of a forest area is damaged in the process of gaining access to and removing one selected high-value tree. In this way, over a period of time, the entire forest will be seriously damaged, even though only relatively few trees have actually been cut down. An equally serious problem is that building access routes into previously dense forest encourages illegal hunters to poach because their work becomes a lot easier. Antelopes, chimpanzees, and gorillas are hunted down and shot for sale as "bushmeat" in the local towns.

Tourists following natives to a village.

TOURISM

Tourists are attracted to African states because of the opportunities to see wildlife and experience novel and dramatic landscapes. Cameroon is able to exploit this tourist market because it benefits from two important assets. First, Cameroon possesses an astonishingly rich ecology that ranges from rainforest to rolling savanna and that includes the most varied flora and fauna in Africa. A second asset is the country's economic and political stability. This makes tourists feel safer in Cameroon than in some of the neighboring states.

Six national parks are open to foreign visitors, and because such visits tend to be expensive, they generate high revenue from a relatively small number of visitors. The plan is to attract up to half a million visitors annually by 2010, though that represents a large increase over the present number of tourists. One of the most well-established and successful parks is Waza National Park, where elephants, antelopes, giraffes, lions, and monkeys roam at will.

A department store in Douala.

OPENING MARKETS

Cameroon aims to develop a free-market economic system while still maintaining a political system that is highly centralized and in control of the national economy. This is often felt to be a difficult challenge because a highly centralized government that seeks to maintain political control may come in conflict with the competing interests of economic groups. The Biya government has had mixed success in managing the economy and controlling the state. One advantage of strong state power is the government is able to offer assurances to foreign companies that their investments will not be ruined by sudden political upheavals. Foreign companies benefit from knowing that their investments will not be nationalized, and this reassurance has enabled Cameroon to attract foreign investment.

As in many African countries, small adverse changes in economic health seriously affect the chances of acquiring the foreign investment essential to finance large-scale ventures. In the mid-1980s, after a downturn in the economy, the World Bank was brought in to provide assistance, and its first move was to insist on budget cuts in government spending.

In recent years the government has started to relax some of its control over the economy. State-owned industries, such as the body that controls the production of palm oil, are being sold to private companies, and there are plans to privatize the cotton industry. Attempts like this to liberalize the economy and encourage private ownership are encouraged by the International Monetary Fund (IMF).

Most of the industry and workers' quarters in Douala are located on the far end of the Wouri Bridge, on the right bank of the Wouri River.

The opening of the all-weather highway from Yaoundé to Douala was gladly welcomed as it provided quick passage between the two cities.

OPENING ACCESS

Improvement of the country's road and transport network plays a major role in supporting new economic ventures and increasing the investment appeal of Cameroon to foreign banks. Poor roads and heavy rainfall in the south have been largely responsible for the inadequacies in the transport system, and this explains why the north has traditionally been isolated from the south. Plans are underway for the construction of a major road between Yaoundé and the western high plateau, as well as other major new roads, and there has been considerable investment in the state railroad system.

Douala, on the estuary of the Wouri River, is the country's main port and accounts for nearly all of Cameroon's shipping trade. Douala also handles shipping trade for Chad and the Central African Republic and uses the region's wide network of rivers for transport to and from these neighboring countries. Minor ports include Limbe, Kribi, which transports logs and cocoa from the interior, and Tiko, which handles the export of bananas, wood, and rubber. In the north traders in the port of Garoua, on the banks of the Bénoué River, transport goods to Nigeria.

There is an international airport at Yaoundé, and Douala and Garoua also handle some local flights. There is an increase in the number of airports in the interior, for example at Tiko, Ngaoundéré, Bafoussam, Bamenda, and Maroua. Cameroon Airlines, which is jointly owned by the government and Air France, handles internal traffic as well as international routes to European and African cities.

The port of Douala is regarded as one of the best-equipped ports in western Africa. It has special docks and equipment for loading wood and minerals.

CAMEROONIANS

CAMEROON HAS A RICH DIVERSITY OF PEOPLE, which makes it more of a cultural crossroads than most other African states. In the north, many people live in a Muslim culture that has been influenced by the Arab world. In the south there is an amalgam of different ethnic groups that is rich and diverse even by African standards. The two dominant groups in Cameroon are the Bamiléké and the Tikar.

BAMILÉKÉ AND TIKAR

The majority of people living in the highlands today are the Bamiléké, although their origins lie to the north of Cameroon. They migrated southwards around the end of the 16th century. The Bamiléké are related to the original Bantus, who are thought to have originated in Cameroon

Left: **A modern woman from Douala.**

Opposite: **Three sisters in casual dress. Nearly half of the population of Cameroon is below 15 years of age.**

49

before spreading across southern Africa. It was the Bantu who first developed the art of working iron and practicing agriculture on an organized scale. Archeological evidence suggests that around 200 B.C., the Bantu began to migrate east and south, developing into the major ethnic group in Africa south of the Sahara. Bantu people now number over 60 million and speak hundreds of languages. The prefix *Ba* in the word Bamiléké is itself a Bantu word meaning "the people of."

Traditionally Bamiléké society was a highly ordered one that ranked people in social classes from the chief down to slaves. Secret societies were also a common feature of Bamiléké societies, and they still operate to some extent, although they are not as powerful as before. The most visible characteristic of the Bamiléké people, however, is their domestic architecture; their thatched homes are a distinctive mark of their cultural presence in modern Cameroon.

The Tikar are similar to the Bamiléké in their lifestyle and art forms, but they claim a separate development from an original group of Tikar people about three centuries ago. Smaller groups that belong to the Tikar people are the Babanki, the Fum, and the Kom. Another of these smaller groups, the Mun, flourished for a short while as an independent kingdom.

THE FULANI

The Fulani are found in most West African states, but most of them live in northern Cameroon. Around A.D. 1000 they moved southward from northern Africa and began to settle along the coast of West Africa. Some of them also moved inland to what is now northern Nigeria. A Muslim people, the Fulani were involved in various *jihads* ("GEE-had"), or holy wars, that saw an extension of their power and influence. In the early 19th century a Fulani empire was established in northern Nigeria and northern Cameroon. This empire was based on an alliance with the Hausa people, and some intermarriages took place between the two groups.

Fulani people live and work as pastoralists, grazing their cattle on the savannas. They also farm and grow crops because this offers some insurance against droughts, which can severely reduce the size and worth of their herds. Their traditional culture attaches a high value to the ownership of cattle: the more animals owned, the higher one's social status.

Above: **Fulani children. When the Muslim Fulani arrived at the Logone valley around A.D. 1000, they managed to convert the people living there to Islam.**

Opposite: **A Bamiléké in festive costume. The Bamiléké live in the larger towns, especially Douala where they are the area's most economically dynamic group.**

Pygmies living in a rainforest. Due to the economic incentive to penetrate the rainforest and build roads for logging purposes, pygmy culture is endangered.

FOREST DWELLERS

In the rainforests of the south live people who have been hunters and gatherers for thousands of years. Popularly known as the pygmies because of their height, these people have an intimate relationship with the forest. It provides them with food and shelter, and their whole culture is influenced by the forest environment. The pygmies live in small hunting bands.

MYRIAD GROUPS

Cameroon has so many minority ethnic groups that together they make up a majority of the country's population. Many of them are Bantu-speaking people who have migrated toward the coastal areas over the centuries. They include the Douala, the Bassa, and the Bakoko.

Another Bantu-speaking tribe is the Bulu. Sometimes referred to as the Boulou, the Bulu are a subdivision of the Fang people who live in Equatorial Guinea and Gabon, as well as Cameroon. The Bulu, who number about half a million in Cameroon, live by hunting and farming and have been influenced by American Protestant missionaries.

In the mountain districts of the northwest, there are various non-Muslim groups that are known collectively as the Kirdi. They include the Bata, the Fali, and Podoko. The term Kirdi, which does not describe any one particular ethnic group, means "people without god" and refers to the fact that they are not Muslims. Thought to have originally come from the east, they gradually retreated farther and farther into the mountains in order to escape more dominant groups like the Fulani and slave-hunting parties.

Near Lake Chad the Choa people lead a seminomadic life. Of Arabic origin, they live in large straw houses with grass roofs and with a separately enclosed bedroom inside the large house. The area outside the inner room, sheltered under a grass roof, acts as a storage area, kitchen, and home for small domesticated animals.

Local cattle owners in Yaoundé.

Older and more conservative people often do not interact with foreigners. Children, however, are more open.

SOCIAL DIFFERENCES

There is a north-south split in Cameroon that tends to create differences between people. As in other African states, the source of the division can be traced back to the historical legacy of colonialism. One important factor in the north-south division is a religious one: the Muslim-dominated north tends to have a different cultural focus from the Christian-dominated south. There are also economic differences because the south, where colonialism had more of an impact, is more advanced in terms of education and economic development. The pace of change in the north is slower.

There is also a social division between Anglophile and Francophile Cameroonians. What used to be French Cameroon, in the east of the country, had a colonial experience that was different from that in British Cameroon. Many people living in what was once British Cameroon were reluctant to find themselves in a unified state with the Francophile east of the country. This division is still apparent in the choice people make to speak French or English.

In northern Cameroon the ethnic group that has been historically the most important is the Fulani. The tension between the Fulani and some minority groups have existed for many generations. In the south, because the Bamiléké forms the majority, ethnic differences are not as distinct.

Cameroon also has nonethnic social divisions that are based on the unequal distribution of wealth in the country. In the larger cities in the south, such as Yaoundé, there are well-educated, sophisticated Cameroonians who have a lifestyle not dissimilar to any wealthy class of people around the world. These people have little in common with the lives of the overwhelming majority of Cameroonians who are not especially well-to-do.

Shops in Cameroon selling French goods.

LIFESTYLE

LIFESTYLES IN CAMEROON reflect the mix of cultural groups living in the country. There are features in most people's lives that cut across the cultural divisions, such as a visit to the weekly market, and because most Cameroonians live and work in the countryside, there are common lifestyle characteristics in this respect as well. In other ways, from the way a house is built to the way one's hair is styled, there are fascinating differences between the cultural groups.

HOMES

In urban centers the structure of buildings is simple. Breeze blocks are used to form the walls and sheets of tin for roofing them. The division between a small town and a large village is not always clear, but a large

Left: **An aerial view of a village in Cameroon.**

Opposite: **A bicycle seller in Maroua. The bicycle is the cheapest form of individual transport in Cameroon.**

A family posing for a photograph in front of their house. Most modern homes have electricity. In rural areas, a lack of electricity means reliance on kerosene to provide fuel for a lamp when night falls.

village will often have different compounds, each one consisting of half a dozen huts with walls made of dried mud and separated by bamboo fences.

A hut rarely stands in isolation, and a village is often simply defined by a compound of homes standing close to one another. In small villages and the countryside, a home is more plainly constructed than a townhouse. The hut is built using mud bricks and a tin roof, with banana plants, mango trees, and shrubs planted in a garden surrounding it. In addition to providing color and shade, these plants produce food for the family. In a patch of bare scrub land close to the home, the family goat will be tethered, and hens and ducks will wander close to their pens.

Villages are often cleaner and neater than an urban compound. In a village each home will have its own latrine. The latrine is actually a deep hole with a large, flat but lightweight stone as a cover, and for privacy a small screen made from the fiber of leaves from palm trees will be used.

A BAMILÉKÉ HOME

The Bamiléké people had the same basic design for their homes for centuries. The main room is square, and the average length of a wall is about 15 feet (4.6 m), while the thatched roof has a distinct conical shape. The walls of the hut are made from mud and bamboo posts. The skill of building is in the construction of a circular platform that rests comfortably and securely on the square walls and supports the conical roof. Creativity and individual style can be seen in the arrangement of palm fronds around the walls of the hut and in the decorative motifs carved on the bamboo posts or on boards around the entrance.

BUILDING A HOME

The building of a traditional home, one that does not consist of just breeze blocks and a tin roof, usually starts by placing slender wooden posts into the ground to form the outer walls. A second row of posts is then placed inside the first square to form the inner walls, and the space in between is filled with layers of raffia palm laid horizontally at intervals of about a foot and tied to the posts at both ends. This provides a structure for the wall, which is then filled and built up with lumps of mud or dried clay. The corners of the square need more support than can be provided by just mud or clay, and hard sticks of raffia are inserted to form a sturdy ribbing for the corner joints. Today bricks or breeze blocks are often used for building the corners of rectangular walls.

The grasslands are home to a variety of plants that provide the raw materials for house building. Mats are made from stalks of millet, which are bunched tightly in clusters and then stuck together in a crisscross pattern. Nails or wire are not needed, and if rope is required to help secure joints, it can be made from the peeled bark of the baobab tree, the fibers of which are pounded together.

House-building is usually reserved for the end of the dry season when there is a lull in agricultural duties and plenty of dry grass to use as material. The roof of a home is often built separately and may be finished and put aside until it is needed. Half a dozen people will then help to hoist the pre-fabricated roof into place. The family will usually celebrate the completion of their new home with a party.

A WOMAN'S LIFE

A Cameroonian woman's life is often more demanding than a man's because she is expected to carry out a range of daily duties that include making trips to the local market for food and pounding the maize to make *fufu* ("PHU-phu"). Fuel for cooking, apart from charcoal which is purchased, comes in the form of small pieces of wood collected from the nearest forest. Equally essential is a daily supply of fresh water, and since very few homes enjoy their own tap water supply, walking to and from the nearest source of water is another daily chore. Women also have the task of looking after their young children and making clothes for them using cloth purchased in the market and an old sewing machine that the family owns.

A man's work responsibilities are restricted to clearing land, getting it ready for a new season's planting of cash crops. The money that is earned is usually kept by the man for his own use.

Different ethnic groups have their own traditions concerning marriage and the role of women. A common practice among many people is for the man to bring a dowry, or bride price, to the parents of the woman he intends to marry. This might take the form of an animal, like an ox. A man can have more than one wife if he can afford a dowry for each of them.

Opposite: **A mother with her twin babies.**

THE *ANLU*

Among the Kom people the *Anlu* is a woman's organization that can be traced back some 300 years. It exists to support social and political issues where women feel they have a contribution to make. In the late 1950s it became actively involved in a local political demonstration. Within a village community, a Kom woman can call upon the *Anlu* if she feels that there is a need. If a man is responsible for a misdeed, such as beating his wife, he can be summoned and asked to apologize or make suitable compensation, depending on the circumstances. There have been cases where a man has repeatedly committed an offense and became the victim of organized public ridicule by the *Anlu* to shame him into a change of behavior.

HAIR WITH STYLE

Women in Cameroon, as in many parts of West Africa, distinguish themselves by taking tremendous care over the style of their hair. Large markets will often have hairstylists, each specializing in a particular manner of braiding the hair. Methods and style of braiding will vary from one part of the country to another, and sometimes it is as popular with men as with women. The braided hair often incorporates the use of beads of varying colors and sizes. These can be threaded onto the hair in highly imaginative ways and contribute a lot to the splendor of many hair styles. Among some Fulani men it is fashionable to have sections of braided hair encased in thin metal strips, preferably bronze, because it can be polished to produce a clear shine.

THE LOCAL MARKET

The local market provides people with the daily necessities of life, such as toothpaste, palm oil, rice, maize flour, and meat. It is best thought of as the African version of a giant supermarket where shoppers can purchase T-shirts, imported shirts and jeans, plastic shoes, thermos flasks, sugar, cloth, cigarettes, beer, cotton, and dried foods.

Market day is a big event in a village or small town, especially for the traders because this is an opportunity to sell their produce for cash. A woman may walk miles to the market to sell just a bag or two of beans she has grown herself. She will set off at dawn from her compound in the hope of securing a prominent place to display her goods. A larger commercial trader will have hired, or will own, a small truck overflowing with a variety of products. The next day he will drive on to another market.

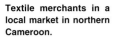
Textile merchants in a local market in northern Cameroon.

OTHER LIFESTYLES

Northern Cameroon is home to several minorities whose lifestyles are gradually adapting to the mainstream life of the country.

In the far north the Kirdi people have a lifestyle that differs from people living in the grasslands, the plateaus, or the rainforest. The Kirdi are a pastoral people who build their farms on the sides of mountains where a system of terracing has evolved over the centuries to make maximum use of the available land. Terrace walls, which follow the natural contours of the land, are carefully maintained by the Kirdi farmers to preserve the physical integrity of each small field.

Close to the border shared with Chad, the Musgum people live around the Logone River, and their dome-shaped homes built of clay are unique. The domes are over 30 feet (9 m) high, and have a small opening at the very top that is only closed during a period of continuous heavy rainfall. The doorways have an unmistakable keyhole shape: narrow at knee-level and then broadening out above this level.

Kirdi people live in round homes built with mud and stone and covered with roofs made from millet straw.

Students as young as 9 may take the Common Entrance Test, and if they are successful, they may begin their secondary education before they turn 10.

EDUCATION

In 1995 there were over 1,000 nursery schools and around 7,000 primary schools with more than 40,000 teachers. The last statistics for secondary education were compiled in 1991, and nearly 20,000 secondary school teachers at 425 schools were registered at that time. There are over 30 teacher training colleges, five institutions of higher education, six universities, and a number of other specialized places of higher learning.

When a child reaches the age of around 11, he or she takes the Common Entrance Test, and the result of this test largely determines what kind of secondary school the child can attend. There is no age limit for the Common Entrance Test. If the results are good, most students and their parents will choose a government school. This is mainly because government schools do not charge any fees. The second choice for students who have unsatisfactory test results, if their families can support them, will be a mission school but these school fees can be too expensive for some families. The third choice is usually a private school, but again there are school fees to pay, and the academic standards vary greatly from one school to another. Some private schools cater to students who failed the Common Entrance Test and need to improve their standard of work.

Around the age of 16, pupils take examinations run by two examination boards, one based on the British system and the other based on the French system. Students may choose which language to take the examinations in though the choice is usually determined by the type and location of the secondary school they attend.

In recent years some schools have experienced funding problems. Thus a number of parent and teacher associations have organized their own methods for collecting funds and hiring extra teachers.

Lively Cameroonian children playing after school.

STAYING IN TOUCH

Cameroon's telephone system is woefully unreliable, being based on analogue telephone centers that are 25 years old. In urban areas the communication system is so outdated that even making a call between the two largest cities, Yaoundé and Douala, can be a painful process. However, both these cities are about to be linked to sophisticated telecommunications complexes that allow mobile phones to make and receive calls from anywhere in the world. This is the first system of its kind in Africa, but whether it is inexpensive enough for people living in remote rural areas remains to be seen. At the moment only a few public telephones exist outside of towns.

In rural areas there are few telephones, so the inadequacies in telephone technology do not affect the lives of most Cameroonians.

PUBLIC TRANSPORTATION

Private transportation is usually used for commercial reasons such as transporting goods and delivering supplies. Apart from a small elite in the large cities, few Cameroonians have their own means of transportation . This does not mean they do not travel regularly; quite the contrary, there is an extensive and inexpensive system of public transportation of cars, minibuses, and small trucks. All of them are popularly called the bush taxi.

Every village and town has its own designated area where bush taxis wait for passengers. There are few scheduled services, other than between the few large cities, and a bush taxi is ready to depart once the seats are full of passengers and their luggage secured on the roof rack overhead. Bush taxis travel to the remotest villages; thus life for most Cameroonians would be unimaginable without them.

Cameroonians on a crowded train. The total length of railway track in the country is 686 miles (1,104 km).

HUMAN RIGHTS

Cameroon has a mixed record on human rights. Tension points emerge when elections are taking place because, despite the democratic infra-structure, the governing party has no intention of releasing its hold on political power. A human rights case that has attracted international attention in recent years concerns Pius Njawé, Cameroon's most famous journalist and editor of the newspaper, *L'Messager*. Published three times a week, this paper has a reputation for high editorial standards, but this did not save its editor from official wrath when he published a critical article about the president.

Cameroonians are reasonably pleased with the country's level of social stability.

PROBLEMS

Although Cameroon's economy is thought to be healthy in some respects, there have also been recent periods of economic hardship. This has resulted in an increase in unemployment, which is causing social problems. School attendance has fallen in some areas, partly because parents cannot afford the fees at mission schools, and partly because the budgets of government schools have been cut back, and there are not enough school facilities and teachers. The crime rate has also increased, and in the far north of the country, it is not unusual for travelers to journey with armed escorts because of the fear of a highway robbery.

About a quarter of rural children are unable to attend school either because their families are poor, or because there are insufficient schools in the neighborhood.

RELIGION

SLIGHTLY MORE THAN half of the population follow traditional African religion, while 33% are Christian, mainly Roman Catholic. The remaining 16% adhere to Islam.

TRADITIONAL RELIGION

Traditional religion is a general name for the indigenous beliefs of African societies. These are not religions in the institutional sense of Christianity and Islam, and there is no set of dogma nor a holy text like the Bible or the Koran ("Koh-ran"). There is, however, the unifying belief that nature is invested with a spiritual force and that there is a need to peacefully coexist with unknown powers. There is a shared sense of continuity between the living and the dead, especially the recent dead,

Left: **The Grand Mosque is the largest mosque in Cameroon. Non-Muslims are not allowed to visit it.**

Opposite: **Muslims congregating outside a mosque at the end of Ramadan.**

To lay members of a community, the diviner is an intermediary between the physical and the spiritual worlds.

and a belief that communication between the two worlds is sometimes possible. That explains why in some parts of Cameroon the deceased are buried in the family home. Some Kirdi groups have soul jars stored in the vicinity of their home so that the dead spirit will have its own home. A soul jar is similar to a small family shrine, and offerings are made on special occasions.

Ancestor-worship is an important aspect of traditional religion. Recently-deceased ancestors are seen as living beings who continue to watch over their family and their village. People take care not to do anything that might offend them, and the shrine of an ancestor will often contain an item once owned by the ancestor.

VERSE FOR THE DECEASED

The underlying respect for life and an affinity with the dead makes itself felt in the first verse of the national anthem of Cameroon.

O Cameroon, thou cradle of our fathers,
Holy shrine where in our midst they now repose,
Their tears and blood and sweat thy soil did water,
On thy hills and valleys once their tillage rose.
Dear fatherland, thy worth no tongue can tell.
How can we ever pay thy due?
Thy welfare we will win in toil and love and peace,
Will be to thy name ever true!

Chorus:
Land of promise, land of glory!
Thou, of life and joy, our only store.
Thine be honor, thine devotion,
And deep endearment, for evermore.

DIVINERS

Diviners are recognized and accepted by the community as possessing special skills that allow them to discover and divine supernatural aspects of life. The attributes that diviners possess are a combination of intuitive knowledge and acquired skills built up over a lifetime of living and working in the community. The sense of the diviner as someone possessing magical and supernatural powers is reinforced by the way in which divination is achieved through special, though often very everyday, means. In western Cameroon, for example, spider divination is practiced using earth spiders, or sometimes the land crab, which lives in an underground burrow. A spider diviner will have a small shrine of his own around the entrance to one of these burrows, and when a villager

A carving on the wall of an ancient shrine.

seeks advice, the diviner will place special cards, inscribed with symbolic markings, inside the burrow. The cards, known as leaf cards because they are made from the leaves of a plum tree, are arranged around some tasty, freshly-acquired insects or some highly edible fresh green leaves that act as bait. In the process of eating the bait, the spider upsets the arrangement of the leaf cards, and it is the new configuration of the cards that the diviner interprets for its message.

Another traditional means of obtaining a reading is to use a crab shell that is filled with wet sand inscribed with symbols and pierced with small sticks. This mixture is poured over a river crab, and after a period of time, the diviner interprets the new configuration of the mixture. The new arrangement of sticks and the mixing up of the symbols represents a communication from a spirit.

CHRISTIANITY

Most Cameroonian Christians are Roman Catholics or Protestants. Groups making up the Protestant faith are Presbyterian, Baptist, and Lutheran. The distribution of Christians and Muslims follows a geographical divide, with more Muslims in the north, while Christians are found in the south of the country.

A church service in a Christian church is likely to be full of music and songs that rely on traditional African rhythms. It is this willingness of Christianity to adapt its practices to harmonize with traditional African religion that accounts for the success of the spread of Christianity across Cameroon and Africa in the 20th century.

A cathedral in Yaoundé.

MISSIONARIES

A Catholic in the prayer garden.

Christianity was first introduced to Cameroon in the first half of the 19th century. One of the earliest recorded interventions was the arrival of the Baptist Missionary Society of London in 1844, and in 1858 land was purchased from a local chief and a religious settlement established. Under German colonial rule, Catholic and Presbyterian groups arrived from Germany and the United States, and there was bitter conflict between the different missions as they jockeyed for influence. They were not, however, allowed to operate in Muslim areas.

Missionaries were initially very intolerant of the beliefs and practices of traditional African religion. New converts were forbidden to dance to traditional village music because it was associated with pagan celebrations. People being introduced to Christianity came to feel ashamed of their own culture and were encouraged to leave it behind. The attitude of missionaries has changed a lot since, and the intolerance has been replaced by an acceptance of many aspects of the traditional way of life.

Muslims have to adhere to the five pillars of Islam. These include professing their faith to Allah, praying five times a day, fasting during the holy month of Ramadan, donating a proportion of one's wealth to the poor, and making a pilgrimage to Mecca at least once during the course of one's life.

BLACK CHURCHES

Until the 1960s the majority of churches remained securely under the control of whites. As congregations grew, so did the need to recruit local people as trained instructors and priests. The development of an African dimension to Christianity was encouraged. Today this reveals itself in the tremendous popularity and spread of independent churches which have adapted their religion to suit African traditions. The role of ancestor worship, polygamy, and traditional medicine were areas of belief that missionaries did not accept, but the new independent churches are more willing to try and integrate these beliefs into their own. Traditional medicine, for instance, overlaps with the notion of faith-healing that is quite common in some evangelical churches, and some churches accept, or turn a blind eye, to the practice of polygamy.

ISLAM

Islam originated in Arabia in the 7th century A.D. and rapidly spread north and west, reaching Tunisia by A.D. 670 and traveling across North Africa and into Spain and Portugal. It was trans-Saharan trade that brought the new religion to West Africa, as Muslim merchants traveled across the caravan routes of the Sahara desert to trade salt for gold from West Africa. What is now northern Nigeria developed important trading centers, and in this way, Islam came to Cameroon.

Islam, which means "submission to God," believes in one god, Allah, and his prophet Mohammed, who was born in Mecca around A.D. 570. Muslims also believe in angels who bring the word of God to ordinary people, and in the 28 prophets who received instruction from God. Jesus Christ was one of these prophets, along with Abraham, David, and Moses.

Ramadan is the most important month of the Muslim year, and its date changes from one year to the next because it is determined by the lunar calendar. During the month of Ramadan, Muslims have to fast, which means they are not allowed to eat or drink between sunrise and sunset.

KEY TERMS OF ISLAM

Hajj ("HAJ") : the pilgrimage to Mecca, one of the five pillars of Islam.

Imam ("ee-MAM") : prayer leader.

Muezzin ("moo-EZ-in") : the person who calls Muslims to prayer by chanting from the mosque's minaret.

Koran ("KOH-ran") : a book containing the sacred words of Allah as revealed to Prophet Mohammed.

Salat ("SAL-at") : worship or act of prayer, carried out five times a day.

Saum ("sow-UM") : fasting, especially during the month of Ramadan.

LANGUAGE

BESIDES FRENCH AND ENGLISH—Cameroon's official languages—the country has a rich linguistic diversity of 24 major African language groups, from at least 200 different ethnic groups. People who live within a few miles of each other may speak different dialects of the same language, which explains why places and people often have more than one name. The Fulani, for example, are also known as the Fula, the Fulanke, the Fulbe, the Fellata, and the Peulh.

FRENCH AND ENGLISH

Of the two official languages, French is more commonly used. English is seldom heard except in the large cities. This is because French Cameroon was a far larger state than British Cameroon. Pidgin English,

Left: **A hairdressing salon in Douala.**

Opposite: **A reporter interviewing a Cameroonian. The government owns all the radio and television stations in Cameroon.**

a simplified version of the English language, is used in Anglophile areas and some Francophile regions. Standard English is rarely used as it is reserved for formal occasions and tends to be spoken only by the highly educated. When Cameroonians find that they do not share a common local language, English or French is used as a practical way of communicating.

A native speaker of English or French would find it difficult to understand what is being said, and they would not be easily understood by the locals in many everyday situations. Most of the African languages spoken in Cameroon are tonal languages, which means the tone of the voice actually changes the meaning of the word. This characteristic spills over to the pronunciation of English and is felt in pidgin English.

PIDGIN ENGLISH

Pidgin English has been spoken in Cameroon for about 300 years, and it is sometimes thought of as a very simplified form of English. This may help explain its origins, but it does not do justice to the complexity of pidgin English, which can be seen as a language in its own right, with its own grammar and vocabulary. Common verbs, such as "is," "have," or "did," are frequently omitted, and the letter "s" is often left off the end of a word. *No tok dat bad people* contains the pidgin word *tok* for "talk" and *dat* for "that;" the sentence expresses a warning about someone else being undesirable company.

A young man, for example, may start a conversation with a woman by asking her where she is going, "*E! Ma sista, usai you di go?*" He may suggest a visit to the local town, "*Make we shake skin for ville.*" The word *ville* comes from French, while *shake skin* is pidgin for "to get going" or "to move."

If someone is asking a companion whether he had a good night's sleep, he may ask, "*You sleep fine?*" or "*Day don clean?*" The word *don*, a familiar

Below: **Women reading in their home. About 63% of Cameroonians are literate.**

Opposite: **French signboards are commonly seen in the eastern part of Cameroon.**

pidgin expression derived from "done," is often used in a variety of situations to express the idea of something completed. For example the sentence, "*I don chop fine*" means "I've eaten well." A *fine chop* means "a hearty meal."

Even within pidgin English there are variations in sentence structure, grammar, and vocabulary. Some linguists use the term "educated pidgin" to describe one type of pidgin English. For example someone may say, "*My friend is my friend*," which means that the subject is a close and trusted friend.

Linguists have compiled pidgin English dictionaries, but the origin of many words and even whole expressions is not always known

Below: **Women singing and enjoying themselves at a party.**

Opposite: **Parents tend to speak pidgin English or dialects to their children at home.**

or understood. For instance it is common to refer to a good friend as "*my combe*" ("kom-BAY"), but it is unknown whether the word *combe* is derived from the English word "comrade" or whether it originates from a local language. What is known is that pidgin English is a highly developed and creative language that cannot be picked up by a native English speaker in a couple of days. Proficient speakers of pidgin English, when traveling across the country, often find new words and expressions that have evolved in one area, and there is a constant process of mixing going on so that the language, like any living language, is always changing.

MASTERS OF LANGUAGE

In Cameroon, because there is no single language used by everyone, switching from one language to the other is common. In the course of one day, Cameroonians may have to use up to six languages. For example they may use English in the former British Cameroon, switch to French when talking to someone from French Cameroon, and converse with market vendors and their family members using the local dialects.

BANTU SPEAKERS

The first Bantu speakers in Africa lived in northern Cameroon for hundreds of years and then, sometime around the first century A.D., began to migrate south. This movement was to have momentous consequences in terms of language. The migration took place gradually over centuries, and as Bantu groups split off from the main population movement and settled down, various Bantu dialects developed. By the year 1500, most of the central, eastern, and southern parts of Africa were inhabited by Bantu-speaking people. These people later migrated south from the Adamawa Plateau toward the coast. About 300 Bantu languages and dialects are now spoken across Africa.

A Bantu-speaking cattle owner. Many minority languages in Cameroon are Bantu-based.

FULFULDE AND BALI

The language of the Fulani is Fulfulde, a member of the Niger-Congo group of West African languages. Fulfulde is quite different from English. The plural of a Fulfulde word is formed by changing the first consonant and the word ending. In English a change to the end of a word is usually sufficient to indicate a plural, but in Fulfulde a plural will often look and sound like a completely different word.

Bali, another local language in Cameroon, was one of the first languages adopted by missionaries in their endeavors to communicate with and convert local people. German missionaries, and later the English, tried to promote Bali as a lingua franca, a common language among speakers of different languages. They also translated the Bible into Bali.

Cameroon is so linguistically diverse that it is not uncommon to find a village or small town having two or even three different names.

SAYING HELLO

A speaker greeting a friend will often say *mia yu* ("ME-ah-u"), but if they are strangers, they may say *mia ka* ("ME-ah-car"). In another local language, Nwe, a person will say "hello" by uttering *alele* ("AL-lay-e") and "goodbye" by wishing the person *go gan bon* ("go-GIN-bon"); the latter expression means "you travel well." The word *bon* is also French for "good," but linguists have argued that this is just a coincidence, and the word is not borrowed from French.

Saying hello to someone is sometimes not a simple matter of uttering one or two words. Like all languages, African ones can be finely tuned to suit the occasion. When two people meet, the relationship and situation may require more than the word "hello." Sometimes, even if the intention is merely to greet one another and say farewell, an outsider might assume they are having a long and meaningful conversation. It would be rude to simply exchange a few words and then separate.

ARTS

CAMEROON IS RICH IN ARTS AND CRAFTS, and this has largely to do with the variety of cultural groups that make up the country. The grasslands region, consisting of numerous small Bantu-speaking societies, is particularly noted for its wooden masks. Besides the Bantu, the Kirdi people are well known for their pottery, and the Tikar are famous for their elaborately decorated brass pipes.

Traditional art is an expression of traditional religious beliefs. When exhibited in museums overseas, many Cameroonian works are not viewed within the context they were created for and therefore are not fully appreciated. Carved human figures are usually created for a special purpose. For example, some were kept near the entrance of a home to guard the place while the family was out working, and small figures of pregnant women were held in the hand during fertility dances.

Left: **A village elder preparing for a ritual. Only the most intricately woven cloth can be used to decorate the ritual table.**

Opposite: **A Fulani artisan carving a calabash. In the Adamawa region the Muslim Fulani are famous for their exquisite work on ornate calabashes.**

87

Above: **A face carving on the door post of a chief's palace.**

Right: **Boys in a masquerade celebrating a festival.**

Opposite: **A woman wearing a bead necklace.**

GRASSLANDS ART

The grasslands is home to the Bamiléké and Tikar people. Their art includes carved masks and figures made from wood and ivory. Popular subjects are human heads, often shown with wide, gaping mouths, and animals such as the elephant, crocodile, snake, panther, and tortoise. The spider, an important creature in divination, is one of the most common motifs used. Carved figures are built onto lavishly decorated house posts in traditional homes. The houseposts stand on either side of the entrance. Domestic items, such as beds and bedposts, bowls, and drinking horns, are also carved with great skill, and the chiefs own elaborately-carved thrones and stools.

In traditional Bamiléké culture only the chief and other high-ranking individuals are permitted to wear an elephant mask during ceremonies

or festivities. The elephant, acknowledged as one of the mighty animals of the land, is a symbol of status and wealth of local chiefs and kings. In some local legends the chief has the magical power to turn himself into an elephant. Accompanying the mask are an elaborate costume, decorated to draw attention to the status of the wearer, and glass beads, which date back to the days of the slave trade when they functioned as a form of currency.

THE BEAUTY OF BEADS

A distinctive art form in Cameroon is the use of beads to decorate wooden sculptures. In past centuries beads were valuable because they were not readily available and only came by way of trade with Nigeria. Beads, like cowries, became a form of currency, and possession of them signified high social status. For this reason the wearing of exquisite bead jewelry and the use of objects decorated with beads were restricted to royal families. Examples of beaded throne stools include a sacred seat used for royal occasions, which has been preserved from this precolonial era. Other beaded items include calabashes, bottles, and pipestems. Modern Cameroonian women also like to wear bead necklaces.

THE AFO-A-KOM

The Kom, one of the small groups making up the Bamiléké people, have an artistic tradition of carving life-sized portraits of their chiefs. When a new chief was formally installed in power, carved effigies of him and the mother of his eldest son were placed outside the palace. The Afo-a-Kom is one of a series of three such beaded sculptures of the Fon Yuh *fons*, a very powerful family credited with semidivine attributes. In the 1960s the Afo-a-Kom was stolen from the Kom capital of Laikon and became international news when it later turned up for sale in New York. Seven years after the theft, it was finally returned to Laikon. The theft brought world attention to the problem of international art theft in Africa. One unexpected consequence of this art theft was to encourage Cameroonians, and the Kom in particular, to treasure their own artistic heritage. Before its disappearance, the Afo-a-Kom was not seen by many Cameroonians, but the world media brought it to their attention. The theft also sparked the interest of Western art collectors in African art.

In the 20th century the art of bead embroidery was developed by self-employed artisans who hoped to sell their work to tourists and other travelers. While the original artisans were employed by royalty, it is now more common for the work to be carried out by groups of village women working in cooperatives. The range of objects that are embroidered with beads is basically the same as it was in the past: bowls, calabashes, and stools, as well as figures of lizards and birds.

The raw materials—cloth, thread, and beads—are purchased by a cooperative from a local market, while the wooden sculpture is commissioned directly from a local woodcarver. The first stage involves cutting cloth to exactly match the sculptured shape. The threaded beads are then sewn onto the cloth. The artist makes sure that there is no space between the individual beads or the rows of beads. The designs are produced from memory or improvised in the course of working. It takes two days to embroider a small object, one week to finish a bird, and three months or more to complete a large calabash. The work is time-consuming because it is all done without the use of any machine, and much care has to be taken to integrate a decorative motif, a spider or a lizard for example, into the pattern. Women complete much of their bead embroidery after the harvest when they have more time to spare.

POTTERY

Pottery fulfills many functions in Cameroon. Special pots are made for ritual occasions celebrating different stages of the life cycle. For example the birth of twins merits a unique Siamese-style pot with two openings at the top.

Some of the most valuable Cameroonian art is pottery crafted solely for the benefit of the local chiefs. These pots are decorated with traditional motifs of animal figures often represented in whimsical poses, such as playfully dancing lizards. Today areas where such pottery was traditionally made are now producing high-quality pottery for export to Europe and the United States.

Beautiful pots are also made for household use. These pots are sold throughout the country. In western Cameroon there is a tradition of making *mimbo* ("MEEM-boh") pots, which have extra large rims to prevent the water or wine inside from spilling. The exterior of these pots are decorated with animals carvings.

Royal compounds like the Bandjoun Palace have been called the last cathedrals of the Bamiléké tradition.

ROYAL ARCHITECTURE

Bamiléké culture is distinguished by its traditional-style village huts. Some of the royal huts, built in the past for their chiefs, still survive till this day. One of the best-preserved and impressive examples of royal architecture is the Bandjoun Palace, located near the town of Bafoussam. It is a large circular compound, over 50 feet (15 m) in circumference, with a second circle of 20-foot-tall (6-m) wooden poles built up outside the compound. These poles support the single thatched roof. Separate huts exist for each of the chief's wives, and all the homes have elaborately decorated doorways. The roads in the palace lead to the village square, which serves as a public area for personal appearances by the *fon* and as the weekly market place.

ZOUK MUSIC

Zouk music is a blend of African and Caribbean music that developed in the 1980s. It has now become one of the most popular musical forms in Cameroon. Zouk music is also well-liked in other parts of western and central Africa. This new genre of music originated in Paris when West Indian bands started to work with and influence musicians from Cameroon and Zaire.

Zouk music first became known outside of Africa and the West Indies when its hi-tech electronic rhythms, which combines African drums with Caribbean percussion, began to dominate the discos of Paris. In terms of musical culture Zouk has a fascinating trajectory because it can be traced back to Africa for its underlying rhythms and harmony and then across the Atlantic to the Caribbean, where it was enriched by European traditions imported by the colonial powers. Now it has returned to West Africa via the musical melting pot of Paris. The important Zouk musicians in Cameroon are Toto Guillaume and Jules Kamga.

MUSIC AND DANCE

As a whole, Cameroon has a rich cultural tradition in music and dance that cannot be categorized. This is partly because many of the different ethnic groups have developed their own distinctive styles of dancing and accompanying music. In the south the xylophone and the drum feature in nearly every band, and many forms of musical theater have developed and incorporated a small orchestra in their performances. In the north Hausa music from Nigeria, characterized by a highly percussive sound and loud drum music, is popular. Francis Bebey is a famous Cameroonian musician and singer who has successfully blended traditional dance rhythms with more modern sounds.

A troupe entertaining an audience with singing and xylophone music.

Cameroon's musical heritage is at its richest in the south because this is where port towns play host to a variety of influences from African and Western countries. One of the first results of this fusion was *asiko* ("A-see-ko") music, which brought together traditional instruments like the xylophone with a Western instrument such as the acoustic guitar. What really swept the country though was *makossa* music, and its enormous popularity lasted through all of the 1970s and the 1980s. Although much of the impetus behind Cameroonian music comes from male bands, female musicians have also made their mark. In the early 1980s Bebe Manga became one of the most successful singers in Africa, and her enchanting songs were hits in French-influenced parts of the West Indies.

Successful Cameroonian musicians include San Fan Thomas and Moni Bile. San Fan Thomas is one of the country's best-known guitarists and is an important figure in the development of Zouk music. Born in 1952 in western Cameroon, his albums include *Funky New Bell*, *Rikiaton*, and *Makassi*. Bile, born in 1957 in Douala, is also a guitarist. His band music fuses popular Cameroonian percussive sounds with rich drum beats from Zaire. His success as a musician arises from his ability to develop the enormously popular *makossa* dance rhythms. This style of music was successfully pioneered in the early 1970s by Manu Dibango, a well-known musician in Cameroon.

ELECTRIC AFRICA

Manu Dibango, born in 1934, is Cameroon's most famous and influential musician. He is now an international star and the best-known Cameroonian musician outside his own country. At the age of 50 his receptiveness to new musical traditions remain undiminished when he recorded a single called *Abele Dance*, which fused African rhythms with those of New York's hip-hop sounds. He went on to produce his own album, *Electric Africa*, which continued to explore ways of joining contemporary electronic music with traditional African rhythms.

Dibango, born in the coastal town of Douala, was 15 when he first went to France to further his studies. He became a saxophonist and pianist and became influenced by the African music coming from Zaire. In 1963 he returned to Cameroon. After a couple of years, he was back in Europe. When he returned to Douala in 1971, he took the country by storm with his hit *Soul Makossa*. This song also became a big hit in the US and turned Dibango into an international attraction.

Manu Dibango has pushed forward the frontiers of African music by opening up its traditional rhythms to modernist musical traditions from Europe and North America. In his own words he wants "to let people know that there is an electric Africa also; that people there are dealing with electricity and with computers. Our music isn't going to be only in museums any more. Because Africa is in the Third World, maybe people are thinking that African musicians aren't able to play pianos, synths or saxes. They want to see Africans beating tomtoms and talking drums...But things are changing."

Albums from Dibango include Deliverance *and* Sweet and Soft. *In* Melodies Africaines, *he performs as a solo pianist. A new version of* Soul Makossa *appears in his 1986 album* Afrijazzy.

Opposite: **A flute player captivates the audience with his playing and dancing. Flute music, whether soothing or lively, is very popular with northern Cameroonians, while South Cameroonians enjoy dramatic music with strong drum beats.**

95

TOBACCO PIPES

Tobacco was introduced to Africa during the 16th century, and pipe-smoking became popular with men and woman. The design of a pipe depended on the social status of the individual, and many of the exquisite examples of carved pipes from Cameroon that are found in museums around the world were made for chiefs. Their elaborately-carved pipes served a ritual purpose and were smoked during fertility festivals. Carved from a variety of materials—clay, metal, gourds, and stone—some of the pipes had skilfully crafted designs decorating the stem and the pot, which holds the tobacco or hemp.

Western Cameroon was noted for its clay pipe-making skills, and many of the finest examples of pipes came from here. Only men manufactured them, and there were rules about what patterns could be inscribed on the pipes. An ordinary person would not be able to afford to have more than a geometric pattern carved on his or her pipe, but a wealthier patron could commission an animal to be carved. Only the chief has the honor to own a pipe carved with human and animal figures.

NOVELISTS

Most Cameroonian novelists write in French, although their work is often translated into English. One of the more famous Francophile writers is Mongo Beti. In his early works, such as *The Poor Christ of Bomba* and *King Lazarus*, Beti exposes the injustices of colonialism and the racist attitudes it fosters. Novelists and other artists are not encouraged to examine contemporary political ills, and censorship tries to ensure that such issues do not appear in print. Beti gets around this problem in his later novels by not setting the stories in Cameroon but creating situations that reflect Cameroonian society.

Beti's novel Perpetua and the Habit of Unhappiness *is recognized as a criticism of the way his country was governed under Ahidjo. This is why this work is banned in Cameroon.*

DRAMA

Conflicts between traditional and modern aspects of cultural life are familiar themes in Cameroonian drama. When young people leave their village community and experience urban life, they are introduced to customs and attitudes that often clash with those they were brought up to believe in. This becomes a source for family conflict when the parents, who adhere to traditional beliefs and customs, cannot understand the way their children have changed. One common scene in dramas is a family arguing about the choice of a husband or wife. Léon-Marie Ayissi's play, *Les Innocents* (The Innocent), deals with problems that arise when a young person seeks to choose his own marriage partner.

A theater performer acting as king of a tribe.

LEISURE

MUSIC, DANCE, AND ENJOYING THE COMPANY of friends and family are defining characteristics in Cameroonian leisure. Gregariousness, as much an African characteristic as it is Cameroonian, lies at the heart of countless festivals and in the way people spend their leisure time. The country is not immune to electronic forms of entertainment: in the cities digital video games are popular. Such imported forms of entertainment, however, have not destroyed the appeal of traditional African games such as *mancala* ("man-KAH-lah").

SOCCER

Soccer is very popular in Cameroon, and interest in the sport is growing due to the success of the national team. Cameroon's team has some of the world's finest players. Since the last two World Cup soccer competitions,

Left: **Cameroon stands a high chance of doing very well in the 2006 World Cup soccer competition. Interest in the game in Cameroon will receive a tremendous boost if South Africa succeeds in winning the nomination for hosting the competition.**

Opposite: **A young boy with his pet monkey.**

Besides soccer and competing in marathons, Cameroonians also like to play table tennis.

they have earned an international reputation for fast-flowing and imaginative play. The team, called the Indomitable Lions, managed to qualify for the quarter finals in the 1990 World Cup. In 1999 Cameroon won the gold medal after beating Zambia in the All-Africa Games.

A RACE UP MOUNT CAMEROON

There is an annual marathon event in Cameroon that attracts many international sportspeople because there is an attractive cash prize. This marathon involves a race to the top of Mount Cameroon. The event takes place in February, and the starting line of over 100 runners is a fraction of the large number who sign up to participate in the 17-mile (27-km) race. More than 50,000 spectators watch the athletes complete the race in under four hours.

THINKING WITH ANIMALS

A fable is a story with a moral. Most African fables revolve around animals. The telling of fables has been part of African culture for centuries, and it continues to this day. Adults and children love to gather in a common village compound to listen to a fable, and the storytelling becomes a shared leisure experience.

The pleasure that people gain from these fables and their function within African society can be best understood when the significance of certain animals is taken into account. A French anthropologist, Claude Lévi-Strauss, said that particular animals are used because they represented important values. Lions, for example, mean courage. Some of the animals used in tales may have become extinct, but that does not lessen their significance in a story because the animals are seen as humans in disguise.

Elephants, as well as leopards, are respected as creatures that control their environment. For this reason they may represent a king or someone with political power in a fable.

Mancala is regarded as one of the earliest two-player strategy games in the world. Despite widespread popularity across most parts of Africa and Asia, it is fairly unknown in Europe and North America.

FABLES FROM CAMEROON

A Fulani Fable About Rewards

In the middle of a night, when mostly everyone was asleep, a man looking at the sky through his telescope spotted a cow hanging from the moon by a long rope. The cow looked healthy and was mooing loudly, so the man called his friend who was a hunter. Carefully aiming his arrow at the hanging rope, the hunter cut through it. The cow fell to earth and landed in a river. Before the hunter could get to the cow, a fisherman caught it by the horns with his fishing line and dragged it to shore, but the cow quickly ran off, attracted by the sound of mooing from a nearby field. The cow joined other cows in the field, and that evening, the farmer stood admiring the new addition to his herd, thinking how lucky he was. This story goes to show that those who do the work don't always get the reward!

A Douala Tale About Two Cats

A man was becoming increasingly worried because his chickens had been disappearing mysteriously from his hen house every night. He suspected the thief was his own cat, but the cat protested her innocence. The man decided to lay a trap. He set up one of his chickens as bait and built a clever trap door that would close and lock in the thief. The next morning, much to his surprise, he found a bushcat inside the trap. From then on, no more of his chickens disappeared. So be careful about accusing someone unless you have some evidence.

A Douala Tale About Strength

The wind liked to blow hard and show off to everyone, "I'm so powerful, I can blow all day and night and at anyone I like. No one is stronger than me." But a small swallow took up his challenge and told him, "Blow as hard as you wish. Birds can still fly." The wind laughed aloud and challenged all the birds to try and resist his power. The hawk was the first to try, but the wind turned into a mighty storm. In the end the struggling hawk gave up. The eagle tried next. Although it could fly very fast, it could not keep up against the wind. Eventually it gave up. The third bird was a heron. It only managed to resist the strong wind for a very short time and finally broke a wing trying. The last bird to meet the wind's challenge was the swallow. Being small, it could dive and dart around and successfully resist the wind. This tale teaches one that strength and skill is not a matter of size, and boasting gets you nowhere.

Women gathered for a
game after a day of work.

MANCALA

Warri ("WAR-ree") is the Cameroonian name for a game that is played
across Africa, especially in West Africa, using a board with two rows of six
holes. Also called *mancala* or *awele* ("a-wee-LEE"), the objective of the
game is to capture the pawns or markers, which are made of seeds,
pebbles, or anything suitable in size, that rest in your opponent's holes in
the board. At either end of the board there is a small cup that collects the
captured pawns for each side.

VILLAGE BARS

Villages usually have a bar serving beer and nonalcoholic juices. The bar
functions as a meeting place for men and women. Millet, sorghum, and
corn can be fermented to make local beer, but today trucks deliver bottled
beer to the most remote corners of the country. In coastal areas people
enjoy palm wine.

Most of the traditional
drums are made by the
village males.

MUSIC

Playing musical instruments, listening to music, and dancing are undetachable elements in Cameroonian leisure activities. People do not simply purchase recordings of their favorite singers or groups and listen to them in the privacy of their homes, as in the West. Music and dance in West Africa is a form of popular public culture, one that people participate in as a group. There is a healthy urban music tradition in Cameroon, but outside of the cities, there are very few professional musicians. Nearly every community has the means to produce music to enliven a social gathering or a special event. The xylophone is one of the most popular instruments and can be easily made using a frame of bamboo placed over gourds that act as resonators for the sound. Drums are also not expensive to make and feature in most village events where music is heard. There are also some more specialized instruments that are not commonly found elsewhere. Women play the *oding* ("oh-DING"), a flute-type instrument that produces light music.

DANCING

Social events everywhere are enlivened by dancing, and urban Cameroon has its own fast-paced dance style called *makossa*. This dance dates back to the 1970s when mission schools used school bands as part of formal school life, for instance, music accompanied the flow of students in and out of daily assemblies.

During the planting season a group of women, as many as 20 or more, will often gather for a drink after a hard day's work in the fields. The village square is a common focal point for such informal parties, and beer is passed around in large gourds. There is often impromptu dancing and singing, with clapping from nonparticipants gathered in a circle.

Two woman happily dancing away. Dance is very much a part of the life of Cameroonians.

FESTIVALS

IN CAMEROON IT IS UNCOMMON to find the kind of national public festivals like Christmas and Thanksgiving that have become institutionalized in Europe and North America. Instead, there is an astonishing diversity of local festivals for an equally diverse set of occasions. Major stages in the life cycle, such as birth, marriage, and death, are celebrated, as are important agricultural events. Yam festivals, for example, take place in parts of southern Cameroon when the yams are ready to be harvested.

FESTIVE OCCASIONS

The death of a chief and the initiation of a new one may be only a local event, but it will be celebrated in a major way. In western Cameroon there is an annual April festival based on the tradition that the tribal chief

Left: **Muslims gathered to celebrate the end of Ramadan.**

Opposite: **A stilt walker in a festive parade.**

These villagers are celebrating a bountiful harvest.

disappears into a cave, only to reappear later, and a ritual procession makes its way to the mouth of the cave. The village priest marks the foreheads of participants with a mixture of camwood and water, and women are blessed for their continued fertility.

Another joyous celebration is the completion of the harvest around the month of February. Harvest festivals are held to ensure fertility of crops and women. In the past a goat would be slaughtered. Different communities will have their own customary practices to celebrate important moments in the agricultural year. Some people place a special pot with an opening at the back in their fields. Small gifts are offered as homage to the god of the field. Before harvest time, to keep animals and birds out of the fields where they can eat the seeds in large quantities, there are many festivals that involve children dressing up with face masks and performing a dance in a field.

FUNERALS

Somber events such as the death of a relative or a friend are considered festive occasions. On the morning of a funeral is the burial, which is a formal event and a show of respect for the relatives of the deceased. The afternoon may be devoted to a community event that includes the family of the deceased. Family members will gather, each person bringing a supply of palm wine that is mixed together in one large *mimbo* pot. Participants then drink from this communal supply as a way of celebrating their oneness, both in honor of the deceased and in acknowledgment that life goes on. In traditional African religion, which influences and even underlies Christian beliefs on the continent, there is a close affinity between the recent dead and the living. A funeral is not regarded as a terminal point of one's life, and this helps explain the festive air that characterizes the afternoon's activities. If the deceased person had a relative or friend who is in a dance society, then the funeral is enlivened by his or her performance. An elaborate funeral can last from between one and three days, and the dancing often goes on through the night.

FANTASIA

Fantasia is an annual traditional celebration that takes place in northern Cameroon. Fantasia can also be celebrated to mark a special occasion, such as the visit of an important person. Visual images of fantasia that are displayed on tourist brochures give the impression that it is a horse-race, but it is not a competitive event. Hundreds of horses can take part, and along with their riders, they are attired in bright and colorful costumes. The whole event is a communal celebration and an occasion for dance and music.

Fantasia is also known as kilizza *("kill-IZZ-r").*

ENSTOOLMENT

For centuries the grassland areas of Cameroon were divided into a rich mosaic of small kingdoms, and each king would have his territory administered by a number of *fons* or chiefs. No longer a formal part of government structure, chiefs continue to play an important part in many rural communities. This is shown by the glamor that characterizes the initiation of a new chief. Special

ceremonies, laid down by custom, are organized and strictly followed. For example Lake Ocu has long been held sacred. When a new chief was enthroned, or enstooled, he was solemnly bathed in the lake's water. An enstoolment, which comes from the symbolic importance of a specially carved seat on which only the king can sit, is the occasion for a major festival. It is marked by large feasts, dramatic dances using traditional dress and masks, and a band performance to provide music for the dances.

THE LELA FESTIVAL

The Lela festival is celebrated annually by the Bali people of western Cameroon. Lasting four days, the festival is held in the month of December. Like all local festivals, it is an important event for members of the community, and Bali people who live and work away from home will make a special effort to return home to join in the festivities. It is a time for families to be reunited and old friends to renew acquaintances. The village chief is the focus of attention during the festival. On the first day he rides on horseback to the local river, where a cock is sacrificed. He is followed by the villagers. All being well, diviners will confirm that the spirits are pleased, and the celebrations can begin. The following days are filled with dances, feasts, and the firing of guns in celebration. All the people wear their finest clothes.

URBAN FESTIVALS

Festivals are as popular in towns as they are in the countryside. In the cities there is a blend of traditional forms of entertainment with modern Western traditions. Cocktail parties often take place in the home among a relatively small number of people.

Just as a village festival takes place in the open space of a compound and involves the whole community, a town festival similarly becomes a public event. A person who has been personally invited by the host family feels free to invite someone else to come along, and the guest may not even have a chance to meet the host during the party. This degree of informality applies to most social events at a public level.

Participants in the Youth Festival parade. Festivals with large-scale celebrations involve a higher degree of planning, as well as applying to the local government office for permission to have a street closed to traffic for the duration of that festival if there is a parade.

111

FOOD

THE MAJORITY OF CAMEROONIANS grow most of the food they eat. There are regional differences in the food they eat because changes in climate affect the kind of crops and vegetables that can be grown. In the south, where rainfall is regular, cassava, plantains, yams, and other root vegetables are a staple of daily meals. In the north the temperature and rainfall is more suitable for the cultivation of maize, sorghum, and millet. There is one common feature throughout the country. Everywhere sauces are made from groundnut paste and palm oil to add taste and flavor to what would otherwise be bland dishes.

VEGETABLES

Cassava is shaped like a carrot, with a brown skin and white flesh. The large tubers are boiled and then pounded into a white paste or flour.

Left: **A family enjoying a drink after dinner.**

Opposite: **A girl on her way to sell bread.**

113

Sometimes cassava is mixed with other vegetables and meat to make a stew. The leaves of the plant are eaten.

Yams are easy to grow if there is sufficient rainfall. Yams are a basic food in many people's diet. The tubers are pounded like cassava and eaten in a variety of ways.

Cocoyams are prepared and eaten in much the same way as yams. Unlike yams, they are tastier and not so bland. Cocoyams thrive in areas of heavy rainfall, such as the tropical rainforest region of Cameroon.

Okra Gumbo is another name for this vegetable that is commonly used in soups and stews because the pods have a thickening effect in the process of being cooked.

Woman cooking cassava. Cassava came originally from South America and is thought to have arrived from there on the returning slave ships. It is now one of the most common vegetables found across West Africa.

Selling grains in a local market.

GRAINS

Sorghum is a valuable corn-like grass that can withstand periods of drought. Sorghum grows up to 13 feet (4 m). The lighter-colored grasses are eaten, while the darker ones are used to make beer.

Millet, a name given to a group of grain grasses that produce small seeds, is able to survive drought and intense heat. Millet thrives in poor soil. It is used to make porridge as well as beer and is pale yellow.

Maize Corn is the more common name for this plant in the United States. Unlike other grains, which came from Asia, maize originated in central and southern America. When the grain is pounded, it produces cornstarch, and the young heads of the plant provide sweet corn.

MEALS

A typical Cameroonian breakfast consists of maize porridge with bread and tea. A meal at lunchtime may have rice with fried plantains or a large omelet, and an evening meal could be boiled yams served with fish or meat, or cooked yams mashed with eggs and eaten with fresh vegetables. If the family can afford to buy meat, beef, chicken, and liver are popular choices. Venison, which is more expensive compared to other meat, tends to be eaten only by wealthier people or during special occasions. Monkeys, dogs, and cats are sometimes hunted for their meat. Chicken mixed with groundnuts and stewed with peppers and onions is a popular dish.

Smoked fish is a popular snack and is usually sold near the docks.

The most common meal consists of *fufu*, a dumpling made from pounded maize or yam flour, and *jammu-jammu* ("JAH-moo-JAH-moo"), a thick stew made from leaves of a local vegetable, with spices and occasionally small pieces of meat added. The local vegetable resembles spinach. *Fufu* is usually shared from a large enamel dish and served with individual plates or bowls of *jammu-jammu*. Small amounts of the *fufu* are taken by hand from the dish and dipped in the bowl of *jammu-jammu*. Main meals are usually eaten with boiled rice, yams, or plantains, and flavor is added to most meals through the use of local vegetables and herbs.

Special meals are reserved for important occasions. Among the Bali people, *shu-a* ("SHOO-r") is made from groundnuts fried with flour. During a wedding feast it is mixed with water and stirred to form a drink for the bridegroom and bride.

Chai-khana ("CHAI-kah-nah") is a teahouse. Mobile *chai-khanas* are common in Cameroon. The vendor will carry two buckets, one of hot water and the other filled with mugs, and a large kettle. Tea is made from cloves and heavily sweetened with sugar. Although cocoa and coffee are also produced in Cameroon, they are not often drunk. The most common hot drink apart from tea is a chocolate-based powder (Ovaltine) mixed with hot water or milk.

EATING ETIQUETTE IN CAMEROON

- Use your right hand only.
- If *fufu* is served, break a piece off before dipping it into the soup or stew.
- Visitors will be offered food first, but be sure not to eat more than a fair share of what is available.
- Don't be surprised if men, women, and children eat separately.
- If a bowl of water is passed around after the meal, wash your fingers in it.

COOKING MEALS

In the countryside, cooking often takes place over a makeshift stove that consists of a small pile of charcoal between a few stones. Although traditional clay pots can still be found, more families now use aluminum pots. A local stream is used for washing dishes.

In cities and larger towns, many families have electric or gas stoves and piped water. In rural areas, people depend on their village well for a supply of fresh water. More villages now have a system to carry water from the well into the village.

A pounder is the most common kitchen implement in both the countryside and in towns because it is essential to the making of *fufu*. When the yam is cooked, it is mixed with water and pounded into a soft ball.

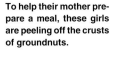

To help their mother prepare a meal, these girls are peeling off the crusts of groundnuts.

STORED FOOD

The need to store food is more important in northern Cameroon than the south. In the southern forest regions, where rainfall is reliable, many crops can be grown through most of the year. In the dryer climate of the north, farmers cannot always take the rain for granted, because some years have a long dry season followed by a short wet one, and this reduces the quantity and quality of the harvest. Many villages have a storage area where surplus food such as yams will survive for most of the year.

Even when a family is growing enough food to feed everyone, canned food is sometimes puchased from the market to add variety to the menu, or when there is a special occasion. Canned sardines are a favorite among many Cameroonians.

A common sight at bus stations, and sometimes at stalls beside a main road, is a woman selling fruit or vegetables. This is usually surplus food grown by a family. Selling it for cash adds to the family income.

A grain store is built to keep food fresh for a long time. Its floor is usually kept above the ground so as to deter insects and animals from reaching the food.

DRINKS

Most Cameroonians prefer to drink tea over coffee. Their favorite tea-drinking places are *chai-khanas*, local teahouses that serve as meeting places for friends to exchange news and gossip. Besides teahouses, a common sight across Cameroon is a large truck making its way by road to small villages to unload crates of soft drinks and Cameroon-brewed beer at the village bar.

Palm wine is a popular alcoholic drink because it is locally made and inexpensive. A farmer may keep dozens of palm trees, planted at different times, so that there is a regular supply of sap available at all times. A small cut is made in the stem, and the sap is collected in a hollowed-out tube

A local bottled drinks factory.

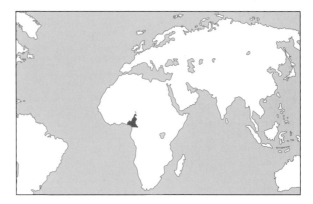

QUICK NOTES

Official Name
Republic of Cameroon

Total Area
180,000 square miles (470,000 square km)

Capital
Yaoundé

Major Cities
Douala, Bamenda, Bafoussam, Maroua

Ports
Douala, Garoua, Kribi, Tiko, Limbe

Highest Point
Mount Cameroon (13,440 feet/4,095 m)

Major Rivers
Bénoué, Logone, Chari, Wouri

Climate
Equatorial, with high temperatures and plentiful rain.

Terrain
Diverse, with coastal lowlands in the south, dissected plateau in the center, mountains in the west, and plains in the north.

Population
15,456,092 (1999 estimate)

Official Languages
French and English

Ethnic Groups
Over 200 ethnic groups, including the Bamiléké, Tikar, Fulani, Douala, Bassa, Bakoko, and Kirdi

Main Religions
Traditional beliefs, Christianity, Islam

Currency
Communaute Financière Africaine franc (CFAF)
US$1 = 575 CFAF (1999)

Natural Resources
Petroleum, bauxite, diamonds, iron ore, timber, hydropower

Main Imports
Machines and electrical equipment, transport equipment, fuel, food

Main Exports
Crude oil and petroleum products, lumber, cocoa beans, aluminium, coffee, cotton

Important Political Leaders
Ahmadou Ahidjo (1961–82), Paul Biya (1982–)

Day of Independence
1 January 1960

GLOSSARY

Anglophile
A person fond of English ways.

breeze blocks
Lightweight blocks made from cinders (breeze), and mixed with cement and sand.

bush taxi
A cheap means of public transport using cars, minibuses, and small trucks.

calabash
A large gourd, used as a container.

camaroes (**"CA-mah-row"**)
A Portuguese word for prawns.

chai-khana (**"CHAI-kah-nah"**)
A teahouse set up in a taxi or bus station.

coup
Sudden, illegal, and violent change of government.

enstoolment
The ceremony to establish a new chief.

fon (**"FOND"**)
The local chief or king.

Francophile
A person enamored of French culture.

fufu (**"phu-phu"**)
A dumpling made from maize or yam flour.

jammu-jammu (**"JAH-moo-JAH-moo"**)
A thick stew made from leaves of a vegetable.

jihad (**"GEE-had"**)
Islamic term for a holy war.

Koran (**"KOH-ran"**)
The Muslim holy book.

mancala (**"man-KAH-lah"**)
A popular two-player African strategy game.

mimbo (**"MEEM-boh"**) **pots**
Pots with a thick rim to prevent spilling, used for holding water or oil.

pastoralists
People who work on farms, tending to animals.

pidgin English
An alternate form of the English language.

Ramadan
The ninth month of the Muslim year, when Muslims fast between sunrise and sunset.

shu-a (**"SHOO-r"**)
A Balinese food, which consists of a mixture made from groundnuts and flour.

BIBLIOGRAPHY

Green, Malcolm. *Through the Year in West Africa.* London: Batsford, 1982.

Harris, Clin. *A Taste of West Africa.* London: Wayland, 1994.

La Duke, Betty. *Africa Women's Art, Women's Lives.* New Jersey: Africa World Press, 1997.

Murphy, Dervla. *Cameroon with Egbert.* London: John Murray, 1989.

Peoples of West Africa. New York: Facts on File Inc., 1989.

INDEX

INDEX

INDEX

PICTURE CREDITS
ANA/J. Du Sordet: 34, 79, 100, 118
ANA/Jean-Guy Jules: 28, 41, 80, 93,
    120
Archive Photos: 29
Björn Klingwall: 7, 8, 11, 23, 32, 39,
    52, 55, 66, 67, 71, 74, 81, 91,
    98, 104, 111
Camera Press: 24, 25, 30
Hutchison Library: 3, 4, 6, 12 (top),
    14, 15, 21, 31, 35, 46, 50, 51, 57,
    58, 64, 65, 69, 70, 77, 82, 83, 84,
    86, 87, 88 (both), 89, 94, 97, 99,
    101, 105, 107, 108, 110, 113, 114,
    116
Jason Laure: 13, 26, 45, 54
North Wind Picture Archives: 20
Topham Picturepoint: 18, 27, 37, 63,
    115, 119
Trip Photographic Agency: 1, 5, 10, 12
    (bottom), 16, 19, 36, 38, 40, 43,
    47, 48, 49, 53, 56, 60, 62, 73, 75,
    78, 103, 106, 112
Victor Englebert: 17, 44, 123